BROWNIES
and
BLONDIES

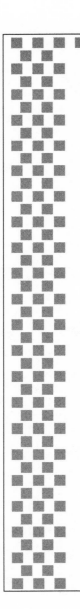

ALSO BY LISA YOCKELSON

The Efficient Epicure
Glorious Gifts from Your Kitchen
Country Pies
Country Cakes
Country Cookies
Fruit Desserts

American Baking Classics

BROWNIES
and
BLONDIES

■ ■ ■

LISA YOCKELSON

HarperCollins*Publishers*

HarperCollins books may be purchased for educational, business, or sales promotional use. For information, please write: Special Markets Department, HarperCollins Publishers, Inc., 10 East 53rd Street, New York, NY 10022.

FIRST EDITION

Designed by Helene Berinsky

Library of Congress Cataloging-in-Publication Data

Yockelson, Lisa.
Brownies and blondies / Lisa Yockelson. — 1st ed.
        p.   cm. — (American baking classics)
                Includes index.
            ISBN 0-06-016751-3 (cloth)
      1. Brownies (Cookery)   I. Title.   II. Series.
                TX771.Y639   1992
          641.8'653—dc20   92–52587

92 93 94 95 96 CG/RRD 10 9 8 7 6 5 4 3 2

to the memory of
the other
Lmy

ACKNOWLEDGMENTS

Throughout the years, friends and colleagues have sustained my study of baking—specifically, homestyle American baking—with interest and enthusiasm. A passion for baking evolved out of my own natural curiosity for the subject. But my love for this area of cooking was spurred on by several editors who, throughout the years, have allowed me the opportunity to explore my ideas in print and to work out formulas for so many delectable things.

It wasn't long before my fascination with baking shaped itself into a definitive project, a series entitled "American Baking Classics." This series, beginning with *Brownies and Blondies*, has come to pass through the tenacious work of Susan Friedland, my editor at HarperCollins, and Susan Lescher, my literary agent. Their collective good sense—and persistence—is not only revealed in the pages that follow, but in the entire working structure of this undertaking. This cookbook, and every volume that follows, is as much theirs as it is mine—so, to each Susan, my appreciation.

Too, I am grateful to the following medley of professionals for their continued support and resourcefulness: Joseph Montebello, creative director at HarperCollins; Karen Mender, vice president and director of marketing at HarperCollins; Bob Kelleter, food editor of the *Washington Post*; Carolyn Larson, assistant to Susan Lescher at Lescher and Lescher, Limited; Patricia Brown, editor and consultant; and Sherri Steinfeld, senior publicist at HarperCollins.

Contents

· 1 ·

All About Brownies and Blondies

THE CLASSIC AMERICAN SWEETS

So very American, brownies hold a time-honored place at charity bake sales, in the holiday cookie tin, heaped on a plate as an after-school treat, or as a casual dessert, simply cut from the baking dish and served forth plain or with a scoop of ice cream.

A pan of brownies resembles a dense, moist, nearly fallen cake—but one that is packed with chocolate. Culinary lore tells the tale of the brownie: it's the story of a cook whose chocolate cake did not rise nearly enough on baking and, not wanting to waste the dessert, the solid piece was cut into small squares and served anyway. And so the delicious mistake became a treasured American sweet.

Thick and lush, brownies can be made chewy, cakelike or fudgy. Brownie mixtures are remarkably tolerant to any number of additions: chopped nuts, marshmallows, coconut, crushed toffee or bittersweet chocolate hand-cut into chunks, alone or in combination, can fortify the dark batter.

Blondies, the amiable cousin of the brownie (also known as blond brownies), are rich in brown sugar and eggs. Most times, the batter is golden-colored and customized with butterscotch or chocolate chips, flaked coconut, oats, chopped nuts or peanut butter.

Brownies and blondies are soft bar cookies, sometimes light and airy, sometimes chewy, and frequently dense and fudgy. Brownies turn a deep brown due to a generous amount of melted unsweetened or milk chocolate, chocolate syrup or unsweetened cocoa powder introduced into the batter. A blondie mixture becomes a butterscotch color due to such prominent ingredients as light brown sugar (or a mixture of brown sugar and granulated sugar) and whole eggs (or a combination of eggs and egg yolks). Chocolate may appear in blondies in the form of chips or chunks.

Of all the bakery goods imaginable, brownies are among the easiest to make. Many of the batters rely on ingredients that most casual cooks have in the pantry and can be put together in the time it takes to preheat the oven. For chocolate lovers, they are a supreme treat. Both brownies and blondies are ideal to keep on hand—a panful can be cut up into squares and stored at room temperature in an airtight tin, or stashed in the freezer for another time.

Most brownies and blondies will keep nicely at room temperature for about one week, or in the freezer for one to two months. Rich brownies, laden with lots of chocolate or cream cheese, should be refrigerated in self-sealing plastic bags or tightly closed containers, with wax paper separating the layers.

The brownies and blondies in this book are meant to be homestyle; that is, they are easy to make as a part of everyday cooking. Even though some brownies may be full of chocolate and fudgy, they are essentially simple. Brownies and blondies are good served as is, or with a sprinkling of confectioners' sugar. However, when nothing else will do except a richly iced brownie, you can spread a dark chocolate icing (see page 24) over almost any uncut brownie cake.

Throughout the years I have established my favorite brownie and blondie recipes. Most are strikingly similar to one another, due in part to a more or less standard set of ingredients—butter, eggs, sugar, chocolate and flour—that figure in each formula. Yet each brownie is special in its own way, given the variations and refinements, added enrichments and flavorings used in a particular recipe. A different texture or taste can be achieved by adding more butter or chocolate, reducing or increasing the amount of flour, butter or eggs, or blending in such ingredients as flavored baking chips or chopped nuts.

ALL ABOUT BAKING BROWNIES AND BLONDIES

Very simply, brownies and blondies are made by combining flour, leavening (if it is used) and spices (for blondies) with a mixture of butter, sugar, eggs, melted chocolate (for brownies) and a spoonful of extract. The resulting batter is at once dense, silky and, sometimes, heavy. Other components that add character to this baked dessert—such as chopped nuts or chocolate chips—get stirred into or sprinkled over the batter at the last moment.

A brownie or blondie batter takes moments to whisk together and turn into a pan, and emerges from the oven about a half hour later, filling the house all the while with the aroma of good baking.

The following observations and techniques, culled from many happy afternoons of baking brownies and blondies, are worth noting, and these instructions go hand in hand with the recipes that make up this book.

Preparing the Baking Pan

To prepare the baking pan, lightly butter the bottom and sides of the pan. Shake a little all-purpose flour over the bottom and sides of the pan to coat it lightly, then tap out the excess flour over the kitchen sink.

Mixing the Batter

Brownie and blondie batters are made in three steps: mixing the dry ingredients, blending together the butter-chocolate-sugar-eggs-flavoring, and combining the liquid and dry ingredients to form a batter.

Unless the directions specifically call for sifting the flour mixture, the flour, leavening and spices can be mixed in a bowl with a spoon, fork or whisk. I use a whisk.

More often than not, both the butter and chocolate are used in the melted state; both should be melted (together, if you like) in a heavy saucepan over very low heat. I use an enameled cast iron saucepan, for in this type of pan the contents melt smoothly without scorching. Draw a spoon through the mixture now and again, then remove the pan from the heat to cool.

Whisk the cooled melted butter and unsweetened chocolate in a large mixing bowl until smooth before beating in the sugar, eggs and flavoring. At this point, the batter might look grainy or even slightly curdled, and this is typical. Sometimes, a very thick chocolate mixture will offer some resistance when stirred and appear "ropy" (or thick and viscous); this is characteristic of certain batters at this stage.

To combine both liquid and dry ingredients, add the flour mixture to the beaten egg mixture and blend it in with a spoon or whisk, mixing until the particles of flour have been absorbed, but avoid overbeating the batter. Scrape down the sides of the bowl once or twice with a rubber spatula to keep the batter even-textured. Most batters will be dense, but still pourable.

Pour and scrape the batter into the prepared pan: it's easiest to angle the mixing bowl over the prepared baking pan and push out the batter with a rubber spatula, scraping the bottom and sides of the bowl as you go. Gently spread the batter to the edges of the pan in an even layer with a flexible palette knife, rubber spatula or small offset metal spatula.

Baking the Brownies and Blondies

All brownies should be baked on the middle level rack of the preheated oven. Brownies and blondies are baked when the top is gently "set." The top will still be somewhat soft (instead of liquidy) and the interior moist. The solid brownie or blondie "cake" will pull away ever so slightly from the edges of the baking pan. Generally, I find that the "toothpick test"— inserting a toothpick into a pan of brownie or blondie batter to check for doneness—is confusing and, now and then, results in overcooked brownies or blondies. (Overbaked brownies, by the way, can be broken up and folded through softened vanilla ice cream or a cheesecake batter—either does a good job of adding moistness to the brownie bits and pieces.)

Thoroughly cool the baked brownies or blondies in the pan on a wire rack. On cooling, some brownies and blondies may sag slightly, forming a slight depression in the center of the baked cake, or the top may crack a jot when cooling—this is traditional and the taste is still superb.

Cutting the Brownies or Blondies into Squares

Once cooled, cut the baked brownies or blondies into squares with a small serrated knife or smooth-bladed knife. A serrated knife works best for cutting all of the dense, chewy blondies and brownies that are loaded with nut, chips, coconut and chopped candy, while a plain-edged knife is handy for cutting through fudgy brownies. Remove the squares or rectangles from the pan with a metal spatula.

INGREDIENTS

Brownies and blondies are made with the basic and familiar ingredients that are a working part of good, everyday baking—butter, flour, sugar, eggs, chocolate, nuts, fruit, spices and flavorings. Here is a checklist of ingredients used in my brownie and blondie recipes:

FLOUR: bleached all-purpose flour; bleached cake flour. Bleached flour produces brownies and blondies with a softer texture.

SUGAR: granulated sugar; light brown sugar (to measure, firmly pack the sugar in a measuring cup used for dry ingredients); superfine sugar, also known as "bar" or "dessert" sugar, is used to create a finer crumb in some of the brownie and blondie batters.

LEAVENING: baking powder; baking soda.

EXTRACTS: pure vanilla extract; pure almond extract; pure orange extract; chocolate extract; coconut extract; peppermint extract.

SPICES: ground cinnamon; ground ginger; ground allspice; whole nutmegs for grating; salt.

BUTTER, SHORTENING AND OIL; CREAM AND MILK: unsalted butter (fresh, not previously frozen); solid shortening; plain vegetable oil; heavy cream; sour cream; evaporated milk; whole milk.

EGGS: All brownie and blondie recipes use extra-large eggs.

CHOCOLATE AND CHOCOLATE CANDY: unsweetened chocolate, available in 1-ounce squares, packaged 8 to a box; pure, unsweetened cocoa powder; semisweet chocolate chips and miniature semisweet chocolate chips (each available in 12-ounce bags); mint-flavored semisweet chocolate chips (available in 10-ounce bags); milk chocolate candy bars (available in 1.55-ounce bars); bittersweet chocolate candy bars (available in 3-ounce bars); chocolate-covered toffee bars (available in 1.4-ounce bars); chocolate-covered peanut butter cups (each 1.8-ounce package contains two peanut butter cups); chocolate-covered raisins (available in 7-ounce bags and in bulk bins, depending upon the market).

NUTS AND SEEDS: walnuts (English walnuts and black walnuts); pecans; macadamia nuts; almonds; roasted peanuts; cashews; roasted sunflower seeds.

Walnuts, almonds and pecans taste best in blondies and brownies when they are lightly toasted; toasting brings out the full flavor of the nuts and improves the finished sweet. To toast the nuts, scatter them on a cookie sheet or jellyroll pan in a single layer and bake in a preheated 350-degree oven for about 5 to 6 minutes. If the nuts are to be sprinkled over the top of a batter, it is unnecessary to toast them first.

PEANUT BUTTER, OATMEAL, RAISINS, DATES AND COCONUT: creamy peanut butter; "quick-cooking" (not instant) oatmeal; dark seedless raisins; golden raisins; moist dried currants; pitted whole dates; sweetened flaked coconut (available in 7-ounce bags).

BUTTERSCOTCH, CARAMEL AND MARSHMALLOWS: butterscotch-flavored chips (available in 12-ounce bags); individually wrapped vanilla caramels (available in 14-ounce bags or in bulk at some markets); miniature marshmallows (available in 6¼-ounce bags); marshmallow cream (available in 7-ounce jars).

Ingredients should be measured out and assembled before you put together a particular recipe. Dairy ingredients should be left at room temperature for a little while to take off the chill.

EQUIPMENT

The brownies and blondies in this book are baked in standard square and rectangular baking pans made of sturdy aluminum. The square pans measure 8-by-8-by-2-inches and 9-by-9-by-2-inches; the rectangular pan measures 13-by-9-by-2-inches. If you have a choice, select pans that have straight sides, rather than curved, sloping sides and corners; in these, the batter bakes into an even cake which is easy to cut into neat squares or rectangles.

STORING BAKED BROWNIES AND BLONDIES

Once the cooled brownie or blondie cake is cut into squares, layer them in a metal cookie tin, separating the layers with sheets of wax paper. Or, individually wrap the brownies or blondies in plastic wrap or clear cellophane, and stack them in the tin. Iced brownies are delicate, and should be arranged in cookie tins in a single layer.

Although brownies rarely linger at my house longer than a few days after baking, they do keep nicely in an airtight container at room temperature. And most brownies can be frozen for several weeks—see pages 9 and 10 for a list of the brownies and blondies that can be made ahead and frozen. Brownies made with cream cheese or sour cream should be kept refrigerated, and brownies made with chopped candy bars or chocolate chips are best refrigerated in the hot and humid summer months.

And remember that rich chocolate brownies, especially the Classic Fudge Brownies (page 16), the Black Bottom Brownies (page 28), Deep Dish Fudge Brownies (page 22), Cream Cheese Brownies (page 46) and the Marbled Vanilla Cheesecake Brownies (page 44) are delicious eaten directly from the freezer.

FREEZING HOMEMADE BROWNIES AND BLONDIES

The following brownies and blondies can be frozen successfully. Wrap the brownies or blondies in sheets of plastic wrap and store them in thick, self-sealing plastic bags designed for the freezer, or in sturdy, freezer-safe storage containers with lids that close tightly. Defrost the brownies or blondies in their wrappings.

Brownies

Black Bottom Brownies (page 28); Chocolate and Orange Brownies (page 54); Chocolate and Raisin Brownies (page 49); Classic Fudge Brownies (page 22); Classic Chewy Brownies (page 18); Cocoa Brownies (page 58); Coffee Chunk Brownies (page 34); Cream Cheese Brownies (page 46); Deep Dish Fudge Brownies (page 22); Double Chocolate Walnut Chunk Brownies (page 26); Marbled Vanilla Cheesecake Brownies (page 44); Milk Chocolate Chunk Brownies (page 33); Mint Brownies (page 38); Mocha Chocolate Chip Brownies (page 35); Peanut Butter and Chocolate Brownies (page 52); Pecan Cream Brownies (page 60); Sour Cream Brownies (page 40); Triple Nut Brownies (page 27).

Blondies

Bittersweet Chocolate and Coconut Blondies (page 85); Cashew and Peanut Butter Blondies (page 74); Chocolate Chip Butterscotch Blondies (page 70); Classic Blondies (page 65); Coconut Blondies (page 68); Golden Pecan Blondies (page 83); Peanut Butter "Candy" Blondies (page 72); Toffee Blondies (page 80).

· 2 ·

Brownies

A pan of brownies seems to celebrate chocolate in all its forms—melted, in chunks and shards, in miniature chips or in nuggets of chopped candy. Whatever the composition of the squares, it's the full-bodied bouquet of chocolate that's highlighted. Frequently, the batter is interrupted by nuts, pieces of bittersweet chocolate, coconut or a silken caramel mixture.

Typical recipes for brownies feature a generous amount of butter and unsweetened chocolate, in addition to assorted flavoring agents. A few batters are fluffy or somewhat fluid, but most are thick, heavy and dark. But once any batter gets turned into a pan and baked, what you pull from the oven is a supremely luxurious, creamy, soft or dense block of chocolate goodness—cakelike, fudgy or chewy, depending upon the recipe.

This collection of brownie recipes, many of them longtime favorites of mine, begins on a nostalgic note—with my paternal grandmother's recipe. Grandma Lilly's brownies are made with all the customary ingredients and, in many ways, her recipe serves as the building block for other formulas, based as it is on the fairly standard amount of ½ pound

(2 sticks) butter, 4 eggs, 4 1-ounce squares (¼ pound) unsweetened chocolate and 2 cups sugar to 1½ cups flour. Other recipes, which are variations on the brownie theme, use more or less chocolate, eggs, flour or sugar.

As an afternoon pick-me-up, offer a plate of brownies with hot or iced coffee, or tall glasses of milk. Or, for a lavish dessert, serve the squares with a fresh strawberry or raspberry compote or hot fudge sauce and a drift of whipped cream.

■ ■ ■

Grandma Lilly's Brownies

This recipe has been adapted from *Country Cookies: An Old-Fashioned Collection* (New York: Harper & Row, 1990), the third in my trilogy of country baking books. Over the years I've amended the recipe by reducing the amount of baking powder from 2 teaspoons to 1 teaspoon and added a little more vanilla to the batter. And lately, I've been using an *unsifted* measurement of cake flour, instead of sifting the flour before measuring it.

My grandmother was famous for these brownies, which she would underbake slightly so that they would remain fudgy, chewy and moist. In this recipe, black walnuts are a distinctive ingredient and they do have a pronounced, slightly musky flavor—you may prefer to substitute the more delicate-tasting English variety. The brownies are delicious either way.

30 1¾-by-2¼-inch brownies

1½ cups unsifted cake flour
1 teaspoon baking powder
½ teaspoon salt
½ pound (2 sticks) unsalted
   butter, melted and cooled
4 squares (4 ounces) unsweetened
   chocolate, melted and cooled

2 cups granulated sugar
4 extra-large eggs
2 teaspoons vanilla extract
½ cup chopped black walnuts

Preheat the oven to 350 degrees. Butter and flour a 13-by-9-by-2-inch baking pan.

Sift together the cake flour, baking powder and salt.

Whisk the butter and chocolate in a bowl; beat in the sugar. Beat in the eggs, one at a time, blending well after each addition. Blend in the vanilla extract. Add the dry ingredients and stir to form a batter. Stir in the walnuts.

Pour and scrape the batter into the prepared pan; spread the batter evenly. Bake the brownies for 23 minutes, or until just set.

Cool the brownies completely in the pan on a rack. Cut into 1¾-by-2¼-inch rectangles. Remove the brownies from the pan using a metal spatula. Store in an airtight tin.

Classic Cake Brownies

The batter for this brownie is made by creaming together the butter, shortening and sugar, then beating in whole eggs, egg yolks and melted chocolate; at last, when the flour is added, the batter has a soft, almost fluffy consistency, very much like a cake frosting. Chocolate chips or chopped nuts are both welcome additions to this brownie batter.

16 2¼-by-2¼-inch brownies

1 cup unsifted all-purpose flour
¼ cup unsifted cake flour
¾ teaspoon baking powder
¼ teaspoon salt
9 tablespoons (1 stick plus 1 tablespoon) unsalted butter, softened
3 tablespoons shortening

1 cup plus 1 tablespoon superfine sugar
2 extra-large eggs
2 extra-large egg yolks blended with 1 tablespoon milk
3 squares (3 ounces) unsweetened chocolate, melted and cooled
1½ teaspoons vanilla extract

Preheat the oven to 350 degrees. Butter and flour a 9-by-9-by-2-inch baking pan.

Sift together the all-purpose flour, cake flour, baking powder and salt.

Cream the butter and shortening in the large bowl of an electric mixer on moderate speed for 2 minutes. Add the sugar and continue beating for 2 minutes. Beat in the eggs, one at a time, blending well after each addition; beat in the egg yolk–milk mixture. On low speed, beat in the melted chocolate and vanilla extract. Add the dry ingredients and beat until the particles of flour are absorbed.

Pour and scrape the batter into the prepared pan; spread the batter evenly. Bake the brownies for 30 minutes, or until just set.

Cool the brownies completely in the pan on a rack. Cut into 2¼-by-2¼-inch squares. Remove the brownies from the pan using a metal spatula. Store in an airtight tin.

VARIATIONS

For *Classic Cake Brownies with Chocolate Chips,* toss ⅔ cup miniature semisweet chocolate chips with 2 teaspoons of the sifted flour mixture. Stir the chocolate chips into the batter after the flour has been added.

For *Classic Cake Brownies with Walnuts or Pecans,* stir ¾ cup chopped nuts into the batter after the flour has been added.

For *Classic Cake Brownies with Nuts and Chips,* toss ½ cup miniature semisweet chocolate chips with 1 teaspoon of the sifted flour mixture. Stir the chocolate chips and ¾ cup chopped walnuts or pecans into the batter after the flour has been added.

NOTE: This recipe is a variation of my mother's cake brownies; while I was growing up, the brownies appeared at school bake sales topped with a dark chocolate icing (the one on page 24) and chopped, lightly toasted walnuts.

Classic Fudge Brownies

These brownies are thin, dark as midnight and chewy-fudgy.

30 1¾-by-2¼-inch brownies

¾ cup unsifted all-purpose flour
¾ cup plus 1 teaspoon unsifted
  cake flour
¼ teaspoon baking powder
¼ teaspoon salt
½ pound plus 2 tablespoons (2
  sticks plus 2 tablespoons)
  unsalted butter, melted and
  cooled

6 squares (6 ounces) unsweetened
  chocolate, melted and cooled
2 cups granulated sugar
4 extra-large eggs
2 extra-large egg yolks
2 teaspoons vanilla extract

Preheat the oven to 350 degrees. Butter and flour a baking pan measuring 13-by-9-by-2-inches.

Thoroughly mix the all-purpose flour, cake flour, baking powder and salt. Whisk the butter and chocolate in a separate mixing bowl; beat in the sugar, eggs, egg yolks and vanilla extract. Add the dry ingredients and stir to form a batter.

Pour and scrape the batter into the prepared pan; spread the batter evenly. Bake the brownies for 25 minutes, or until just set.

Cool the brownies completely in the pan on a rack. Cut into 1¾-by-2¼-inch rectangles. Remove the brownies from the pan using a metal spatula. Store in an airtight tin.

NOTE: These brownies are so moist that they must be cut carefully with a small, sharp serrated knife. Wipe off the knife blade each time you cut a new row.

VARIATION

For *Classic Fudge Brownies with Walnuts, Almonds or Roasted Peanuts,* stir 1 cup chopped nuts into the batter after the flour has been added.

Classic Chewy Brownies

This brownie has a moist, exceptionally chewy quality and deep, dark color. Typical of extra-chewy brownies, there are few eggs in the batter, and the sweet bakes into thin squares. These brownies freeze very well.

30 1¾-by-2¼-inch brownies

1¼ cups unsifted all-purpose flour
3 tablespoons unsifted cake flour
⅔ cup unsweetened cocoa
¼ teaspoon baking soda
¾ teaspoon salt
2 cups granulated sugar

⅔ cup vegetable oil
¼ cup plus 1 tablespoon water
¼ cup milk
2 teaspoons vanilla extract
1 extra-large egg
1 extra-large egg yolk

Preheat the oven to 350 degrees. Butter and flour a 13-by-9-by-2-inch baking pan.

Sift together the all-purpose flour, cake flour, cocoa, baking soda, salt and sugar into a bowl. Add the oil, water, milk, vanilla extract, egg and egg yolk. Stir to form a batter. The batter will be dark, somewhat shiny and moderately thick.

Scrape the batter into the prepared pan; spread the batter evenly. Bake the brownies for 25 minutes.

Cool the brownies completely in the pan on a rack. Cut into 1¾-by-2¼-inch rectangles. Remove the brownies from the pan using a metal spatula. Store in an airtight tin.

VARIATIONS

For *Classic Chewy Brownies with Walnuts, Pecans, Roasted Peanuts or Almonds*, sprinkle 1 cup chopped nuts on top of the batter just before baking.

For *Classic Chewy Brownies with Chocolate Chips*, stir ½ cup chocolate chips into the sifted mixture, then add the oil, water, milk, vanilla extract, egg and egg yolk.

For *Classic Chewy Brownies with Nuts and Chocolate Chips*, stir ½ cup chocolate chips into the sifted mixture, mix in the oil, water, milk, vanilla extract, egg and egg yolk, then stir in ⅔ cup chopped nuts.

Chocolate, Walnut and Caramel Brownies

These chocolate brownies are treated to a swirl of caramel and a generous sprinkling of chopped walnuts. They would be a delicious addition to a holiday sweet table, picnic or brown bag lunch.

16 2¼-by-2¼-inch brownies

¼ pound (about 12) vanilla-
  flavored caramels
3 tablespoons heavy cream
½ cup plus 2 tablespoons unsifted
  all-purpose flour
2 tablespoons unsifted cake flour
¼ teaspoon salt
10 tablespoons (1 stick plus 2
  tablespoons) unsalted butter,
  melted and cooled

3 squares (3 ounces) unsweetened
  chocolate, melted and cooled
1 cup granulated sugar
3 extra-large eggs
1½ teaspoons vanilla extract
¾ cup chopped walnuts

Preheat the oven to 350 degrees. Butter and flour a 9-by-9-by-2-inch baking pan.

Slowly heat the caramels and cream in a saucepan until melted, stirring now and again. Cool slightly.

Thoroughly mix the all-purpose flour, cake flour and salt.

Whisk the butter and chocolate in a bowl; beat in the sugar, eggs and vanilla extract. Add the dry ingredients and stir to form a batter. Stir ½ cup of the batter into the caramel mixture.

Pour and scrape the chocolate batter into the prepared pan; spread the batter evenly. Spoon over the chocolate-caramel mixture and swirl it in with a small spatula or table knife. Sprinkle the walnuts on top. Bake the brownies for 25 minutes, or until just set.

Cool the brownies completely in the pan on a rack. Cut into 2¼-by-2¼-inch squares. Remove the brownies from the pan using a metal spatula. Store in an airtight tin.

Deep Dish Fudge Brownies

These chewy-fudgy brownies are thicker than the Classic Fudge Brownies on page 16. The batter is sturdy enough to trap such additions as chopped nuts, chocolate chips, coconut or bits of crunchy toffee.

16 2¼-by-2¼-inch brownies

¾ cup unsifted all-purpose flour
¾ cup unsifted cake flour
¼ teaspoon baking powder
¼ teaspoon salt
½ pound (2 sticks) unsalted butter, melted and cooled

4 squares (4 ounces) unsweetened chocolate, melted and cooled
1¾ cups superfine sugar
4 extra-large eggs
2 teaspoons vanilla extract

Preheat the oven to 350 degrees. Butter and flour a 9-by-9-by-2-inch baking pan.

Sift together the all-purpose flour, cake flour, baking powder and salt.

Whisk the butter and chocolate in a bowl; beat in the sugar, eggs and vanilla extract. Add the dry ingredients and stir to form a batter.

Pour and scrape the batter into the prepared pan; spread the batter evenly. Bake the brownies for 30 to 33 minutes, or until just set.

Cool the brownies completely in the pan on a rack. Cut into 2¼-by-2¼-inch squares. Remove the brownies from the pan using a metal spatula. Store in an airtight tin.

VARIATIONS

For *Deep Dish Fudge Brownies with Chocolate Chips*, toss ½ cup miniature semisweet chocolate chips with 1½ teaspoons of the flour mixture. Stir the chocolate chips into the batter after the flour has been added.

For *Deep Dish Fudge Brownies with Bittersweet Chocolate*, toss 1 bar (3 ounces) bittersweet chocolate, chopped, with 1 teaspoon of the flour mixture. Stir the chocolate into the batter after the flour has been added.

For *Deep Dish Fudge Brownies with Walnuts, Almonds or Pecans*, stir ¾ cup chopped nuts into the batter after the flour has been added. An additional ½ cup chopped nuts may be scattered on top of the batter.

Chocolate and Macadamia Brownies with Dark Chocolate Icing

The soft icing that glosses over these macadamia-speckled brownies is my version of my mother's frosting; this is the frosting that she always spread over the Cake Brownies on page 14. (My mother used a little more vanilla extract and butter.) It's easily mixed in a bowl and is so good spread over plain or nut-flecked brownies. The secret to its success is to beat the mixture steadily for 6 or 7 minutes, so that the sugar dissolves completely and the icing increases in volume.

16 2-by-2-inch brownies

FOR THE BROWNIES:

¼ cup plus 2 tablespoons unsifted all-purpose flour
2 tablespoons unsifted cake flour
¼ teaspoon salt
5 tablespoons unsalted butter, melted and cooled

2 squares (2 ounces) unsweetened chocolate, melted and cooled
1 cup granulated sugar
2 extra-large eggs
½ teaspoon vanilla extract
½ cup chopped macadamia nuts

FOR THE DARK CHOCOLATE ICING:

3 squares (3 ounces) unsweetened chocolate, melted but still warm
⅓ cup plus 1 teaspoon superfine sugar
¼ cup unsifted confectioners' sugar

½ cup heavy cream, warmed slightly
Pinch of salt
½ teaspoon vanilla extract
2 tablespoons unsalted butter, softened

Preheat the oven to 350 degrees. Butter and flour an 8-by-8-by-2-inch baking pan.

For the brownies, thoroughly mix the all-purpose flour, cake flour and salt.

Whisk the butter and chocolate in a bowl; beat in the sugar, eggs and vanilla extract. Add the dry ingredients and macadamias, and stir to form a batter.

Pour and scrape the batter into the prepared pan; spread the batter evenly. Bake the brownies for 25 minutes, or until just set.

Cool the brownies completely in the pan on a rack.

For the dark chocolate icing, blend the chocolate, superfine sugar, confectioners' sugar, heavy cream, salt, vanilla extract and butter in the small bowl of a standing mixer. Beat for 6 to 7 minutes on moderately high speed, or until the icing is smooth and thick, and every granule of sugar has dissolved. (A hand-held mixer can be used to make this icing, too; add an extra 1 to 2 minutes to the beating time.) Spread the icing over the brownies, swirling it as you go.

Let the brownies stand for at least an hour to firm up the frosting. Cut into 2-by-2-inch squares. Remove the brownies from the pan using a metal spatula. Store the brownies in a single layer in airtight tins.

Double Chocolate Walnut Chunk Brownies

These candylike brownies are full of chocolate.

16 2¼-by-2¼-inch brownies

¾ cup unsifted all-purpose flour
⅓ cup unsifted cake flour
1 tablespoon unsweetened cocoa
¼ teaspoon salt
1 bar (3 ounces) bittersweet chocolate (such as Lindt Excellence or Tobler Tradition), coarsely chopped
3 squares (3 ounces) unsweetened chocolate, melted and cooled

12 tablespoons (1 stick plus 4 tablespoons) unsalted butter, melted and cooled
1⅓ cups granulated sugar
4 extra-large eggs
1 teaspoon vanilla extract
½ cup chopped walnuts

Preheat the oven to 350 degrees. Butter and flour a 9-by-9-by-2-inch baking pan.

Sift together the all-purpose flour, cake flour, cocoa and salt. Toss the chocolate with 1 teaspoon of the flour mixture.

Whisk the melted chocolate and butter in a bowl; beat in the sugar, eggs and vanilla extract. Add the dry ingredients, chopped chocolate and walnuts, and stir to form a batter. The batter will be fairly stiff.

Pour and scrape the batter into the prepared pan; spread the batter evenly. Bake the brownies for 28 minutes, or until just set.

Cool the brownies completely in the pan on a rack. Cut into 2¼-by-2¼-inch squares. Remove the brownies from the pan using a metal spatula. Store in an airtight tin.

Triple Nut Brownies

Using a good Dutch-process cocoa for these brownies adds a full rounded chocolate flavor to the baked sweet. Other combinations of chopped nuts can be used, such as almonds, hazelnuts and brazil nuts, or pecans, black walnuts and English walnuts. For a richer dessert, top the brownies with the dark chocolate icing on page 24.

16 2¼-by-2¼-inch brownies

1¼ cups unsifted all-purpose flour	2 cups granulated sugar
¼ cup unsweetened cocoa	1½ teaspoons vanilla extract
¼ teaspoon salt	½ teaspoon almond extract
½ pound (2 sticks) unsalted butter, melted and cooled	4 extra-large eggs
	⅓ cup chopped walnuts
4 squares (4 ounces) unsweetened chocolate, melted and cooled	⅓ cup chopped pecans
	⅓ cup chopped almonds

Preheat the oven to 350 degrees. Butter and flour a 9-by-9-by-2-inch baking pan.

Sift together the all-purpose flour, cocoa and salt.

Whisk the chocolate and butter in a bowl; beat in the sugar, vanilla extract, almond extract and eggs. Add the dry ingredients and nuts, and stir to form a batter.

Pour and scrape the batter into the prepared pan; spread the batter evenly. Bake the brownies for 30 minutes, or until just set.

Cool the brownies completely in the pan on a rack. Cut the brownies into 2¼-by-2¼-inch squares. Remove the brownies from the pan using a metal spatula. Store in an airtight tin.

Black Bottom Brownies

A cream cheese and chocolate chip topping that traditionally graces black bottom cupcakes is delicious spooned over a plain brownie batter just before baking. What you pull from the oven is a rich, fudgy, confectionlike brownie—wonderful as a teatime treat or dessert.

16 2¼-by-2¼-inch brownies

FOR THE BROWNIES:

¾ cup unsifted all-purpose flour
¼ teaspoon baking powder
¼ teaspoon salt
8 tablespoons (1 stick) unsalted butter, melted and cooled
3 squares (3 ounces) unsweetened chocolate, melted and cooled

1 cup superfine sugar
2 extra-large eggs
1 extra-large egg yolk
2 teaspoons vanilla extract

FOR THE CREAM CHEESE TOPPING:

2 3-ounce packages cream cheese, softened
¼ cup granulated sugar
Pinch of salt

1 extra-large egg
¼ teaspoon vanilla extract
½ cup miniature semisweet chocolate chips

Preheat the oven to 350 degrees. Butter and flour a 9-by-9-by-2-inch baking pan.

For the brownies, thoroughly mix the all-purpose flour, baking powder and salt. Set aside 2 teaspoons of the flour mixture for the cream cheese topping.

Whisk the butter and chocolate in a bowl; beat in the sugar, eggs, egg yolk and vanilla extract. Add the dry ingredients and stir to form a batter.

Pour and scrape the batter into the prepared pan; spread the batter evenly.

For the cream cheese topping, beat the cream cheese, sugar and salt in a bowl on moderate speed for 2 minutes. Add the egg and vanilla extract and beat for 1 minute. Toss the chocolate chips with the reserved 2 teaspoons of dry ingredients and stir into the cream cheese mixture. Pour the topping over the brownie batter; gently swirl the cream cheese mixture into the chocolate batter using a table knife or small spatula. Bake the brownies for 30 to 32 minutes, or until just set.

Cool the brownies completely in the pan on a rack. Cut into 2¼-by-2¼-inch squares. Remove the brownies from the pan using a metal spatula. Refrigerate in an airtight tin.

Rocky Road Brownies

Bumpy with bits and pieces of pecans, miniature marshmallows and chocolate chips, these brownies bake up moist and rich.

16 2¼-by-2¼-inch brownies

¾ cup unsifted all-purpose flour
2 teaspoons unsweetened cocoa
¼ teaspoon salt
½ cup semisweet chocolate chips
8 tablespoons (1 stick) unsalted
   butter, melted and cooled
2 squares (2 ounces) unsweetened
   chocolate, melted and cooled

¾ cup superfine sugar
2 extra-large eggs
½ teaspoon vanilla extract
¾ cup miniature marshmallows
½ cup chopped pecans

Preheat the oven to 350 degrees. Butter and flour a 9-by-9-by-2-inch baking pan.

Sift together the all-purpose flour, cocoa and salt. Toss the chocolate chips with 1 teaspoon of the flour mixture.

Whisk the butter and melted chocolate in a bowl; beat in the sugar, eggs and vanilla extract. Add the dry ingredients and stir to form a batter. Stir in the marshmallows, pecans and chocolate chips.

Pour and scrape the batter into the prepared pan; spread the batter evenly. Bake the brownies for 25 minutes, or until just set.

Cool the brownies in the pan on a rack. Cut into 2¼-by-2¼-inch squares. Remove the brownies from the pan using a metal spatula. Store in an airtight tin.

VARIATION

For *Coconut Rocky Road Brownies*, add ¼ cup sweetened flaked coconut to the batter along with the chips and nuts.

Raspberry-Chocolate Brownies

All-natural raspberry preserves, prepared without additional sugar, is best for this brownie recipe. The preserves have a clear, fresh fruit flavor. These brownies are dense and fudgy.

16 2¼-by-2¼-inch brownies

1 cup plus 2 tablespoons unsifted all-purpose flour
¼ teaspoon salt
10 tablespoons (1 stick plus 2 tablespoons) unsalted butter, melted and cooled
5 squares (5 ounces) unsweetened chocolate, melted and cooled

1¼ cups granulated sugar
2 extra-large eggs
2 extra-large egg yolks
½ teaspoon vanilla extract
½ cup raspberry preserves

Preheat the oven to 350 degrees. Butter and flour a 9-by-9-by-2-inch baking pan.

Thoroughly mix the all-purpose flour and salt. Whisk the butter and chocolate in a bowl; beat in the sugar, eggs, egg yolks and vanilla extract. Add the dry ingredients and stir to form a batter.

Pour and scrape two-thirds of the batter into the prepared pan; spread the batter evenly. Blend the preserves into the remaining batter and pour on top. Swirl the raspberry mixture into the all-chocolate batter with a small spatula or table knife. Bake the brownies for 25 to 27 minutes, or until just set.

Cool the brownies completely in the pan on a rack. Cut into 2¼-by-2¼-inch squares. Remove the brownies from the pan using a metal spatula. Store in an airtight tin.

Milk Chocolate Chunk Brownies

Pools of milk chocolate and chopped pecans wind through this brownie batter. Simple and cakelike, the baked squares are particularly good for packing up in the picnic hamper as a pick-up dessert. Have a bowl of fresh cherries, nectarines or plums on hand for eating along with the brownies.

16 2¼-by-2¼-inch brownies

1 cup unsifted all-purpose flour
3 tablespoons unsifted cake flour
¼ teaspoon baking soda
¼ teaspoon salt
1 bar (1.55 ounces) milk chocolate, chopped
8 tablespoons (1 stick) unsalted butter, melted and cooled

2 bars (1.55 ounces each) milk chocolate, melted and cooled
¾ cup superfine sugar
2 extra-large eggs
½ teaspoon vanilla extract
½ teaspoon chocolate extract
⅓ cup chopped pecans

Preheat the oven to 350 degrees. Butter and flour a 9-by-9-by-2-inch baking pan.

Thoroughly mix the all-purpose flour, cake flour, baking soda and salt. Toss the chopped chocolate with 1½ teaspoons of the flour mixture.

Whisk the butter and melted chocolate in a bowl; beat in the sugar, eggs, vanilla extract and chocolate extract. Add the dry ingredients and stir to form a batter. Stir in the chopped chocolate and pecans.

Pour and scrape the batter into the prepared pan; spread the batter evenly. Bake the brownies for 25 minutes, or until just set.

Cool the brownies completely in the pan on a rack. Cut into 2¼-by-2¼-inch squares. Remove the brownies from the pan using a metal spatula. Store in an airtight tin.

Coffee Chunk Brownies

Laced with chopped almonds and chunks of toffee candy, these brownies are a pleasant companion to cups of espresso or hot chocolate.

16 2¼-by-2¼-inch brownies

¾ cup unsifted all-purpose flour
¼ teaspoon baking powder
¼ teaspoon salt
3 bars (1.4 ounces each) chocolate-covered almond toffee candy, chopped
7 tablespoons unsalted butter and 1 teaspoon instant coffee, melted together and cooled

3 squares (3 ounces) unsweetened chocolate, melted and cooled
¾ cup superfine sugar
1 extra-large egg
2 extra-large egg yolks
1 teaspoon vanilla extract
¼ teaspoon almond extract
½ cup chopped almonds

Preheat the oven to 350 degrees. Butter and flour a 9-by-9-by-2-inch baking pan.

Thoroughly mix the all-purpose flour, baking powder and salt. Toss the toffee with 2 teaspoons of the flour mixture.

Whisk the butter-and-coffee mixture and melted chocolate in a bowl; beat in the sugar, egg, egg yolks, vanilla extract and almond extract. Add the dry ingredients and stir to form a batter. Stir in the toffee candy.

Pour and scrape the batter into the prepared pan; spread the batter evenly. Sprinkle the almonds on top. Bake the brownies for 25 minutes, or until just set.

Cool the brownies completely in the pan on a rack. Cut into 2¼-by-2¼-inch squares. Remove the brownies from the pan using a metal spatula. Store in an airtight tin.

Mocha Chocolate Chip Brownies

These make a good base for individual hot fudge brownie sundaes: warm the brownie squares (if you like), place each on a deep plate and top with a scoop of vanilla ice cream and a ladle of hot fudge.

16 2¼-by-2¼-inch brownies

⅔ cup unsifted all-purpose flour
¼ teaspoon salt
½ cup miniature semisweet chocolate chips
10 tablespoons (1 stick plus 2 tablespoons) unsalted butter and
1½ teaspoons instant coffee granules, melted and cooled

5 squares (5 ounces) unsweetened chocolate, melted and cooled
1¼ cups granulated sugar
2 extra-large eggs
1 extra-large egg yolk
1½ teaspoons vanilla extract

Preheat the oven to 350 degrees. Butter and flour a 9-by-9-by-2-inch baking pan.

Thoroughly mix the all-purpose flour and salt. Toss the chocolate chips with 1 teaspoon of the flour mixture.

Whisk the butter-and-coffee-mixture and melted chocolate in a bowl; beat in the sugar, eggs, egg yolk and vanilla extract. Add the flour and chocolate chips, and stir to form a batter.

Pour and scrape the batter into the prepared pan; spread the batter evenly. Bake the brownies for 25 minutes, or until just set.

Cool the brownies completely in the pan on a rack. Cut into 2¼-by-2¼-inch squares. Remove the brownies from the pan using a metal spatula. Store in an airtight tin.

Mud Brownies

It's the delicious muddle of marshmallow cream and chocolate icing that gives these sweet, toothsome brownies their name.

30 1¾-by-2¼-inch brownies

FOR THE BROWNIES:

1¼ cups unsifted flour
2 tablespoons unsifted cake flour
3 tablespoons unsweetened cocoa
¼ teaspoon salt
½ pound (2 sticks) unsalted butter, melted and cooled

4 squares (4 ounces) unsweetened chocolate, melted and cooled
1¾ cups granulated sugar
4 extra-large eggs
1 teaspoon vanilla extract

FOR THE "MUD" TOPPING:

1 7-ounce jar marshmallow cream (see note below)
2 recipes dark chocolate icing (see page 24)

1 cup chopped walnuts, lightly toasted

Preheat the oven to 350 degrees. Butter and flour a 13-by-9-by-2-inch baking pan.

For the brownies, sift together the all-purpose flour, cake flour, cocoa and salt.

Whisk the butter and chocolate in a bowl; beat in the sugar, eggs and vanilla extract. Add the dry ingredients and stir to form a batter.

Pour and scrape the batter into the prepared pan; spread the batter evenly. Bake the brownies for 25 minutes, or until just set. Cool the brownies in the pan on a rack for 5 to 10 minutes.

For the "mud" topping, spread the marshmallow cream over the still-warm brownies. Cool the brownies for 45 minutes. Spread the chocolate icing in large patches over the marshmallow cream; the marshmallow cream and icing will blend together in patches here and there, creating a muddy effect. Sprinkle the walnuts on top.

Cool the brownies completely in the pan on a rack. Cut into 1¾-by-2¼-inch rectangles. Remove the brownies from the pan using a metal spatula. Store in an airtight tin.

NOTE: Marshmallow cream is available in 7-ounce jars in the baking section of most supermarkets.

Mint Brownies

Mint-flavored chocolate chips flavor this thin, chewy brownie. Bite-size squares are wonderful to nibble on with iced coffee or tea.

16 2-by-2-inch brownies

¾ cup unsifted all-purpose flour
¼ teaspoon salt
⅔ cup mint-flavored chocolate chips
6 tablespoons unsalted butter, melted and cooled

3 squares (3 ounces) unsweetened chocolate, melted and cooled
1 cup superfine sugar
2 extra-large eggs
¼ teaspoon peppermint extract
¼ teaspoon vanilla extract

Preheat the oven to 350 degrees. Butter and flour an 8-by-8-by-2-inch baking pan.

Thoroughly mix the all-purpose flour and salt. Toss the chocolate chips with 2 teaspoons of the flour mixture.

Whisk the butter and chocolate in a bowl; beat in the sugar, eggs, peppermint extract and vanilla extract. Add the dry ingredients and stir to form a batter. Stir in the chocolate chips.

Pour and scrape the batter into the prepared pan; spread the batter evenly. The batter will cover the pan in a thin layer. Bake the brownies for 22 to 25 minutes, or until just set.

Cool the brownies completely in the pan on a rack. Cut into 2-by-2-inch squares. Remove the brownies from the pan using a metal spatula. Store in an airtight tin.

VARIATION

For *Mint Brownies with Walnuts, Pecans or Almonds*, stir ½ cup chopped nuts into the batter along with the mint-flavored chips.

Sour Cream Brownies

This is a good bake sale brownie—the squares stay exceptionally moist for at least a week in a tightly sealed tin, and need nothing more than a sprinkling of confectioners' sugar just before packaging.

16 2-by-2-inch brownies

¾ cup unsifted all-purpose flour
1 tablespoon unsweetened cocoa
¼ teaspoon baking powder
¼ teaspoon salt
⅓ cup miniature semisweet
   chocolate chips
5 tablespoons unsalted butter,
   melted and cooled

3 squares (3 ounces) unsweetened
   chocolate, melted and cooled
1 cup granulated sugar
2 extra-large eggs
¼ cup sour cream
1 teaspoon chocolate extract
1 teaspoon vanilla extract

Preheat the oven to 325 degrees. Butter and flour an 8-by-8-by-2-inch baking pan.

Sift together the all-purpose flour, cocoa, baking powder and salt. Toss the chocolate chips with 1 teaspoon of the sifted mixture.

Whisk the butter and unsweetened chocolate in a bowl; beat in the sugar and eggs. Beat in the sour cream, chocolate extract and vanilla extract. Add the dry ingredients and stir to form a batter. Stir in the chocolate chips.

Pour and scrape the batter into the prepared pan; spread the batter evenly. Bake the brownies for 27 to 30 minutes, or until just set.

Cool the brownies completely in the pan on a rack. Cut into 2-by-2-inch squares. Remove the brownies from the pan using a metal spatula. Store in an airtight tin.

VARIATIONS

For *Sour Cream Brownies with Walnuts or Pecans*, stir ½ cup chopped nuts into the batter along with the miniature chocolate chips.

For *Sour Cream Brownies with Coconut*, stir ⅓ cup sweetened flaked coconut into the batter along with the miniature chocolate chips.

Chocolate Brownies with Coconut and Pecan Topping

Offer scoops of vanilla or coconut ice cream with these brownies, or serve them plain, with hot or iced coffee.

16 2-by-2-inch brownies

FOR THE BROWNIES:

1 cup unsifted cake flour
¼ teaspoon baking soda
¼ teaspoon salt
8 tablespoons (1 stick) unsalted butter, melted and cooled
3 squares (3 ounces) unsweetened chocolate, melted and cooled

1 cup granulated sugar
2 extra-large eggs
1 teaspoon vanilla extract
½ teaspoon coconut extract (optional)
½ cup sweetened flaked coconut

FOR THE COCONUT-PECAN TOPPING:

⅓ cup sweetened flaked coconut
½ cup chopped pecans

1 tablespoon evaporated milk

Preheat the oven to 350 degrees. Butter and flour an 8-by-8-by-2-inch baking pan.

Thoroughly mix the cake flour, baking soda and salt.

Whisk the butter and the chocolate in a bowl; beat in the sugar, eggs, vanilla extract and coconut extract, if you are using it. Add the dry ingredients and stir to form a batter. Stir in the ½ cup coconut.

Pour and scrape the batter into the prepared pan; spread the batter evenly.

For the coconut-pecan topping, toss the coconut, pecans and evaporated milk in a bowl. Sprinkle on top of the batter.

Bake the brownies for 25 minutes, or until just set.

Cool the brownies completely in the pan on a rack. Cut into 2-by-2-inch squares. Remove the brownies from the pan using a metal spatula. Store in an airtight tin.

Marbled Vanilla Cheesecake Brownies

For these brownies, a walnut-flecked cream cheese mixture winds through a deluxe brownie batter. Adding a half cup of chopped bittersweet chocolate or miniature semisweet chocolate morsels to the vanilla cheesecake makes a lavish brownie.

16 2¼-by-2¼-inch squares

FOR THE VANILLA CHEESECAKE:

2 3-ounce packages cream cheese, softened

2 tablespoons unsalted butter, softened

3 tablespoons granulated sugar

2 extra-large egg yolks

¼ teaspoon vanilla extract

2 teaspoons unsifted cake flour

¼ cup chopped walnuts

FOR THE BROWNIES:

¾ cup unsifted all-purpose flour

¼ cup unsifted cake flour

¼ teaspoon baking powder

¼ teaspoon salt

12 tablespoons (1 stick plus 4 tablespoons) unsalted butter, melted and cooled

3 squares (3 ounces) unsweetened chocolate, melted and cooled

1½ cups granulated sugar

3 extra-large eggs

1½ teaspoons vanilla extract

Preheat the oven to 350 degrees. Butter and flour a 9-by-9-by-2-inch baking pan.

For the vanilla cheesecake, beat the cream cheese, butter and sugar in a small bowl with a hand-held beater on moderate speed for 2 minutes; beat in the egg yolks, vanilla extract and cake flour. Stir in the walnuts. Set aside.

For the brownies, thoroughly mix the all-purpose flour, cake flour, baking powder and salt.

Whisk the butter and chocolate in a bowl; beat in the sugar, eggs and vanilla extract. Add the dry ingredients and stir to form a batter.

Pour and scrape *half* of the brownie batter into the prepared pan. Top with large spoonfuls of the vanilla cheesecake batter. Pour and scrape the remaining brownie batter on top; level the top with a spatula. Draw a table knife (or flexible palette knife) through the batter to create swirls. Bake the brownies for 35 minutes, or until just set.

Cool the brownies completely in the pan on a rack. Cut into 2¼-by-2¼-inch squares. Remove the brownies from the pan using a metal spatula. Refrigerate in an airtight tin.

Cream Cheese Brownies

These cakelike brownies are rich, moist, and creamy-textured—they taste like a feathery chocolate cheesecake. Serve the brownies, dusted with confectioners' sugar, along with a compote of fresh raspberries.

30 1¾-by-2¼-inch brownies

1 cup unsifted all-purpose flour
½ cup unsifted cake flour
¼ teaspoon baking powder
¼ teaspoon salt
¼ cup miniature semisweet
  chocolate chips
2 3-ounce packages cream cheese,
  softened

8 tablespoons (1 stick) unsalted
  butter, softened
1⅓ cups granulated sugar
4 extra-large eggs
4 squares (4 ounces) unsweetened
  chocolate, melted and cooled
2 teaspoons vanilla extract

Preheat the oven to 350 degrees. Butter and flour a 13-by-9-by-2-inch baking pan.

Sift together the all-purpose flour, cake flour, baking powder and salt. Toss the chocolate chips with 2 teaspoons of the flour mixture.

Beat the cream cheese and butter in the large bowl of an electric mixer on moderately high speed for 3 minutes. Add the sugar and beat for 2 minutes. Add the eggs, one at a time, beating well after each addition. Add the chocolate and vanilla extract and beat on low speed for 1 minute. Add the dry ingredients and mix until the particles of flour are absorbed. The batter will be very light and fluffy, almost like stiffly whipped heavy cream. Stir in the chocolate chips.

Scrape the batter into the prepared pan; spread the batter evenly. Bake the brownies for 25 minutes, or until just set.

Cool the brownies completely in the pan on a rack. Cut into 1¾-by-2¼-inch rectangles. Remove the brownies from the pan using a metal spatula. Refrigerate in an airtight tin.

VARIATION

For *Cream Cheese Brownies with Walnuts, Pecans, Almonds or Macadamia Nuts*, stir 1 cup chopped nuts into the batter along with the chocolate chips.

Toasted Almond and Coconut Brownies

This brownie batter is enriched with shreds of flaked coconut, toasted almonds and Amaretto. Just before serving, dust the tops of the brownies with sifted confectioners' sugar.

30 1¾-by-2¼-inch brownies

1 cup unsifted all-purpose flour
½ teaspoon salt
½ pound (2 sticks) unsalted
  butter, melted and cooled
5 squares (5 ounces) unsweetened
  chocolate, melted and cooled
1¾ cups superfine sugar

4 extra-large eggs
1½ tablespoons Amaretto
1 teaspoon almond extract
1 cup chopped almonds, lightly
  toasted
1 cup sweetened flaked coconut

Preheat the oven to 350 degrees. Butter and flour a 13-by-9-by-2-inch baking pan.

Thoroughly mix the all-purpose flour and salt.

Whisk the butter and chocolate in a bowl; beat in the sugar, eggs, Amaretto and almond extract. Add the dry ingredients and stir to form a batter. Stir in the almonds and coconut.

Pour and scrape the batter into the prepared pan; spread the batter evenly. Bake the brownies for 23 minutes, or until just set.

Cool the brownies completely in the pan on a rack. Cut into 1¾-by-2¼-inch rectangles. Remove the brownies from the pan using a metal spatula. Store in an airtight tin.

Chocolate and Raisin Brownies

These brownies are dense and moist. For a change, you can substitute chocolate-covered raisins or chocolate-covered peanuts for the plain raisins.

16 2-by-2-inch brownies

⅔ cup unsifted cake flour
2 tablespoons unsweetened cocoa
¼ teaspoon salt
¾ cup dark raisins
8 tablespoons (1 stick) unsalted butter, melted and cooled

3 squares (3 ounces) unsweetened chocolate, melted and cooled
1 cup granulated sugar
1 extra-large egg
2 extra-large egg yolks
1 teaspoon vanilla extract

Preheat the oven to 350 degrees. Butter and flour an 8-by-8-by-2-inch baking pan.

Sift together the cake flour, cocoa and salt. Toss the raisins with 2 teaspoons of the flour mixture.

Whisk the butter and chocolate in a bowl; beat in the sugar, egg, egg yolks and vanilla extract. Add the dry ingredients and stir to form a batter. Stir in the raisins.

Pour and scrape the batter into the prepared pan; spread the batter evenly. Bake the brownies for 25 minutes, or until just set.

Cool the brownies completely in the pan on a rack. Cut into 2-by-2-inch squares. Remove the brownies from the pan using a metal spatula. Store in an airtight tin.

Brown Sugar, Almond and Chocolate Brownies

The brown sugar adds an elusive caramel flavor to these almond-speckled brownies. Hot or iced coffee would be the ideal beverage to serve.

16 2¼-by-2¼-inch brownies

⅔ cup unsifted all-purpose flour
⅓ cup unsifted cake flour
¼ teaspoon baking powder
½ teaspoon salt
5 tablespoons unsalted butter, melted and cooled
3 squares (3 ounces) unsweetened chocolate, melted and cooled

⅔ cup light brown sugar
⅓ cup granulated sugar
1 extra-large egg
1½ teaspoons vanilla extract
1 cup sliced almonds

Preheat the oven to 350 degrees. Butter and flour a 9-by-9-by-2-inch baking pan.

Thoroughly mix the flours, baking powder and salt.

Whisk the butter and chocolate in a bowl; beat in the light brown sugar, granulated sugar, egg and vanilla extract. Add the dry ingredients and stir to form a batter. Stir in ¾ cup of the almonds.

Pour and scrape the batter into the prepared pan; spread the batter evenly. Sprinkle the remaining almonds on top. Bake the brownies for 27 to 30 minutes, or until just set.

Cool the brownies completely in the pan on a rack. Cut into 2¼-by-2¼-inch squares. Remove the brownies from the pan using a metal spatula. Store in an airtight tin.

Milk Chocolate Brownies with Peanuts, Cashews and Raisins

Nutty and soft, these brownies are a fine mid-afternoon treat. For even richer brownies, add ½ cup milk chocolate chips to the batter.

16 2¼-by-2¼-inch brownies

⅔ cup unsifted cake flour
1 tablespoon unsweetened cocoa
¼ teaspoon salt
½ cup dark raisins
6 tablespoons unsalted butter, melted and cooled
2 bars (1.55 ounces each) milk chocolate, melted and cooled

½ cup granulated sugar
1 extra-large egg
1 teaspoon vanilla extract
½ cup chopped peanuts
½ cup chopped cashews

Preheat the oven to 350 degrees. Butter and flour a 9-by-9-by-2-inch baking pan.

Sift together the cake flour, cocoa and salt. Toss the raisins with 1½ teaspoons of the flour mixture.

Whisk the butter and chocolate in a bowl; beat in the sugar, egg and vanilla extract. Add the dry ingredients, raisins, peanuts and cashews and stir to form a batter.

Pour and scrape the batter into the prepared pan; spread the batter evenly. Bake the brownies for 20 to 25 minutes, or until just set.

Cool the brownies completely in the pan on a rack. Cut into 2¼-by-2¼-inch squares. Remove the brownies from the pan using a metal spatula. Store in an airtight tin.

Peanut Butter and Chocolate Brownies

Dense and fudgy, and thoroughly dotted with chocolate chips and chopped peanuts, these brownies are a good dessert cookie to serve with freshly brewed coffee or hot chocolate.

30 1¾-by-2¼-inch brownies

1 cup unsifted all-purpose flour
2 tablespoons unsifted cake flour
¼ teaspoon baking powder
¼ teaspoon salt
½ cup miniature semisweet
　chocolate chips
12 tablespoons (1 stick plus 4
　tablespoons) unsalted butter,
　melted and cooled
1 cup semisweet chocolate chips
　and 2 squares (2 ounces)
　unsweetened chocolate, melted
　and cooled

¾ cup granulated sugar
¼ cup light brown sugar
¾ cup creamy peanut butter
3 extra-large eggs
2 extra-large egg yolks
1½ teaspoons vanilla extract
1 cup chopped peanuts

Preheat the oven to 350 degrees. Butter and flour a 13-by-9-by-2-inch baking pan.

Thoroughly mix the all-purpose flour, cake flour, baking powder and salt. Toss the chocolate chips with 2 teaspoons of the flour mixture.

Whisk the butter and melted chocolates in a bowl; beat in the granulated sugar and brown sugar. Beat in the peanut butter until thoroughly combined. Beat in the eggs, one at a time; blend in the egg yolks and vanilla extract. Add the dry ingredients and stir to form a batter. Stir in the chocolate chips.

Pour and scrape the batter into the prepared pan; spread the batter evenly. Sprinkle the peanuts on top. Bake the brownies for 25 minutes, or until just set.

Cool the brownies completely in the pan on a rack. Cut into 1¾-by-2¼-inch rectangles. Remove the brownies from the pan using a metal spatula. Store in an airtight tin.

Chocolate and Orange Brownies

The sprightly flavor of orange adds a bright edge to these fudgelike brownies. Homemade candied orange peel, coarsely chopped, can be added to the batter in place of the grated citrus peel.

16 2-by-2-inch brownies

1 teaspoon freshly grated orange
  peel
½ teaspoon orange extract
¼ cup unsifted all-purpose flour
3 tablespoons unsifted cake flour
3 tablespoons unsweetened cocoa
¼ teaspoon salt
5 tablespoons unsalted butter,
  melted and cooled

3 squares (3 ounces) unsweetened
  chocolate, melted and cooled
1 cup granulated sugar
1 extra-large egg
2 extra-large egg yolks
1 tablespoon thawed orange juice
  concentrate

Preheat the oven to 350 degrees. Butter and flour an 8-by-8-by-2-inch baking pan.

Combine the orange peel and extract in a small bowl.

Sift together the all-purpose flour, cake flour, cocoa and salt.

Whisk the butter and chocolate in a bowl; beat in the sugar, egg, egg yolks and orange juice concentrate. Blend in the orange peel mixture. Add the dry ingredients and stir to form a batter.

Pour and scrape the batter into the prepared pan; spread the batter evenly. Bake the brownies for 20 to 22 minutes, or until just set.

Cool the brownies completely in the pan on a rack. Cut into 2-by-2-inch squares. Remove the brownies from the pan using a metal spatula. Store in an airtight tin.

NOTE: To make candied orange peel, wash and dry one thick-skinned orange (such as a navel). Cut the orange into wedges and peel away the flesh. Cut the peel into large dice, place in a saucepan of cold water and bring to a boil. Boil for 1 minute; drain. Repeat the process twice more, placing the peel in cold water, bringing it to the boil and boiling for 1 minute. Refresh the peel in cold water, draining it well. In a heavy saucepan, place 1 cup water and 1 cup granulated sugar, cover and cook over low heat until the sugar dissolves completely. Uncover, bring to the boil, boil 5 minutes, add the peel, and simmer until the peel is quite tender and glazed over, about 15 to 20 minutes. Transfer the peel to a small stainless steel sieve to drain. Let the peel cool on a plate. Refrigerate the glazed peel in a covered container for up to 3 weeks.

Old-Fashioned Chocolate Syrup Brownies

Brownies made with chocolate syrup are soft and cakelike. When I was a child, my mother frequently made a variation of this recipe for grade school bake sales. Top the brownies with a sprinkling of confectioners' sugar just before serving or packing up.

30 1¾-by-2¼-inch brownies

⅔ cup unsifted all-purpose flour
⅓ cup plus 2 teaspoons unsifted
    cake flour
¼ teaspoon baking powder
½ teaspoon salt
10 tablespoons (1 stick plus 2
    tablespoons) unsalted butter,
    softened

¾ cup superfine sugar
4 extra-large eggs
2 teaspoons vanilla extract
1 cup chocolate syrup
1¼ cup chopped walnuts

Preheat the oven to 350 degrees. Butter and flour a 13-by-9-by-2-inch baking pan.

Sift together the all-purpose flour, cake flour, baking powder and salt.

Beat the butter in the large bowl of an electric mixer on moderate speed for 2 minutes. Add the sugar and beat for 2 minutes longer. Beat in the eggs, one at a time, blending well after each addition. Beat in the vanilla extract and chocolate syrup. The mixture will look curdled. On low speed, blend in the sifted ingredients. Stir in ¾ cup walnuts.

Pour and scrape the batter into the prepared pan; spread the batter evenly. Sprinkle the remaining walnuts on top. Bake the brownies for 28 minutes, or until just set.

Cool the brownies completely in the pan on a rack. Cut into 1¾-by-2¼-inch rectangles. Remove the brownies from the pan using a metal spatula. Store in an airtight tin.

VARIATION

For Old-Fashioned Chocolate Syrup Brownies with Almonds, substitute 1¼ cups chopped almonds for the walnuts.

Cocoa Brownies

Brownies made with cocoa have a deep, dark chocolate flavor—these are cakelike but moist, and are best eaten very fresh.

30 1¾-by-2¼-inch brownies

1 cup unsifted all-purpose flour
½ cup unsifted cake flour
⅔ cup unsweetened cocoa
½ teaspoon baking powder
¾ teaspoon salt
½ pound (2 sticks) unsalted
  butter, melted and cooled

2 cups granulated sugar
4 extra-large eggs
1½ teaspoons vanilla extract
2 tablespoons evaporated milk

Preheat the oven to 350 degrees. Butter and flour a 13-by-9-by-2-inch baking pan.

Sift together the all-purpose flour, cake flour, cocoa, baking powder and salt.

Whisk the butter and sugar in a large bowl; beat in the eggs, vanilla extract and evaporated milk. Add the sifted ingredients in 2 additions, beating until the particles of flour are absorbed.

Pour and scrape the batter into the prepared pan; spread the mixture evenly. Bake the brownies for 25 to 28 minutes, or until just set.

Cool the brownies completely in the pan on a rack. Cut into 1¾-by-2¼-inch rectangles. Remove the brownies from the pan using a metal spatula. Store in an airtight tin.

VARIATIONS

For *Cocoa Brownies with Walnuts or Pecans*, stir 1 cup chopped nuts into the batter after the sifted ingredients have been added.

For *Cocoa Brownies with Chocolate Chips*, toss ⅔ cup miniature semi-sweet chocolate chips with 2 teaspoons of the sifted ingredients. Stir the chips into the batter after the sifted ingredients have been added.

Pecan Cream Brownies

A good splash of heavy cream smooths out a batter enriched with both cocoa and unsweetened chocolate. This is a luxury brownie, reminiscent of fudge cake.

30 1¾-by-2¼-inch brownies

1¼ cups unsifted all-purpose flour
¼ cup unsweetened cocoa
¼ teaspoon baking powder
½ teaspoon salt
½ pound (2 sticks) unsalted
   butter, melted and cooled
4 squares (4 ounces) unsweetened
   chocolate, melted and cooled

2 cups granulated sugar
4 extra-large eggs
1 extra-large egg yolk
2 teaspoons vanilla extract
¼ cup heavy cream
1 cup chopped pecans

Preheat the oven to 350 degrees. Butter and flour a 13-by-9-by-2-inch baking pan.

Sift together the all-purpose flour, cocoa, baking powder and salt.

Whisk the butter and chocolate in a bowl; beat in the sugar, eggs, egg yolk and vanilla extract. Blend in the heavy cream. Add the dry ingredients and stir to form a batter. Stir in the pecans.

Pour and scrape the batter into the prepared pan; spread the batter evenly. Bake the brownies for 25 minutes, or until just set.

Cool the brownies completely in the pan on a rack. Cut into 1¾-by-2¼-inch rectangles. Remove the brownies from the pan using a metal spatula. Store in an airtight tin.

VARIATION

For *Walnut, Almond, Cashew, or Macadamia Cream Brownies*, substitute 1 cup chopped nuts for the pecans.

Brown Butter—Walnut Brownies

For these brownies, the butter is cooked to a tawny brown color before it is mixed with the chocolate, sugar and eggs; the nutlike flavor of the browned butter adds depth to the chocolate batter. Serve the brownies with freshly brewed coffee or espresso.

16 2-by-2-inch brownies

10 tablespoons (1 stick plus 2 tablespoons) unsalted butter
⅔ cup plus 2 tablespoons unsifted all-purpose flour
3 tablespoons unsweetened cocoa
¼ teaspoon salt
3 squares (3 ounces) unsweetened chocolate, melted and cooled

1 cup granulated sugar
1 extra-large egg
2 extra-large egg yolks
½ teaspoon vanilla extract
¾ cup chopped walnuts

Preheat the oven to 350 degrees. Butter and flour an 8-by-8-by-2-inch baking pan.

Place the butter in a saucepan, set over low heat and cook until melted; raise the heat to moderately high and cook until a medium brown color. Set aside to cool.

Sift together the all-purpose flour, cocoa and salt.

Whisk the butter and chocolate in a bowl; beat in the sugar, egg, egg yolks and vanilla extract. Add the dry ingredients and stir to form a batter. Stir in the walnuts.

Pour and scrape the batter into the prepared pan; spread the batter evenly. Bake the brownies for 30 minutes, or until just set.

Cool the brownies completely in the pan on a rack. Cut into 2-by-2-inch squares. Remove the brownies from the pan using a metal spatula. Store in an airtight tin.

· 3 ·

Blondies

Cream-colored and moist, blondies taste of brown sugar, butter and vanilla. Blondie batters are given body and substance by the addition of oatmeal, flaked coconut, chopped nuts, creamy peanut butter or a stir-in of chocolate chips or chopped bittersweet chocolate bars. Oatmeal, one of my favorite additions to a blondie batter, creates a soft but substantial blondie. And spices, especially cinnamon or freshly grated nutmeg, add a full, rounded flavor to the baked squares.

Blondies are appealing in the summer, served with icy glasses of lemonade, limeade and freshly pressed fruit drinks, or in the fall and winter, with apple cider, mulled wine or hot coffee. Bowls of homemade applesauce, ice cream or a light fruit compote are all good accompaniments.

Classic Blondies

The golden-colored batter, speckled with butterscotch morsels, flaked coconut and chopped walnuts, bakes up into a rich, chewy sweet. Serve the blondies all by themselves or with a plain fruit dessert, such as applesauce.

16 2¼-by-2¼-inch blondies

¾ cup plus 2 tablespoons unsifted
   all-purpose flour
½ teaspoon baking powder
¼ teaspoon salt
½ cup butterscotch chips
8 tablespoons (1 stick) unsalted
   butter, melted and cooled

¾ cup light brown sugar
¼ cup granulated sugar
1 extra-large egg
1 extra-large egg yolk
1 teaspoon vanilla extract
⅔ cup sweetened flaked coconut
¾ cup chopped walnuts

Preheat the oven to 350 degrees. Butter and flour a 9-by-9-by-2-inch baking pan.

Thoroughly mix the all-purpose flour, baking powder and salt in a bowl. Toss the butterscotch chips with 2 teaspoons of the flour mixture.

Whisk the butter, brown sugar, granulated sugar, egg, egg yolk and vanilla extract in a bowl. Pour the butter-sugar mixture over the dry ingredients, add the butterscotch chips, coconut and walnuts, and stir to form a batter.

Pour and scrape the batter into the prepared pan; spread the batter evenly. Bake the blondies for 25 minutes, or until just set.

Cool the blondies completely in the pan on a rack. Cut into 2¼-by-2¼-inch squares. Remove the blondies from the pan using a metal spatula. Store in an airtight tin.

Classic Peanut Butter Blondies

This is a soft, chewy blondie which is delightful served in the summertime with freshly pressed lemonade. And if you are in the mood to be extravagant, serve the blondies *à la mode*, with scoops of vanilla ice cream.

16 2¼-by-2¼-inch blondies

1 cup unsifted all-purpose flour
2 tablespoons unsifted cake flour
¼ teaspoon baking powder
¼ teaspoon baking soda
¼ teaspoon salt
½ teaspoon ground cinnamon
½ teaspoon freshly grated nutmeg
6 tablespoons unsalted butter,
   softened

¾ cup light brown sugar
¼ cup superfine sugar
⅔ cup creamy peanut butter
2 extra-large eggs
1 teaspoon vanilla extract
1 tablespoon milk
¾ cup chopped peanuts

Preheat the oven to 350 degrees. Butter and flour a 9-by-9-by-2-inch baking pan.

Thoroughly mix the all-purpose flour, cake flour, baking powder, baking soda, salt, cinnamon and nutmeg.

Beat the butter, light brown sugar and superfine sugar in the large bowl of an electric mixer on moderate speed for 2 minutes. Beat in the peanut butter. Blend in the eggs, vanilla extract and milk. Stir in the dry ingredients and peanuts.

Pour and scrape the batter into the prepared pan; spread the batter evenly. Bake the blondies for 30 minutes, or until just set.

Cool the blondies completely in the pan on a rack. Cut into 2¼-by-2¼-inch squares. Remove the blondies from the pan using a metal spatula. Store in an airtight tin.

VARIATION

For *Classic Peanut Butter Blondies with Butterscotch Chips*, toss ¾ cup butterscotch chips with 1½ teaspoons of the flour mixture and add to the batter along with the peanuts.

Coconut Blondies

Chewy, and full of the flavor of brown sugar and coconut, these blondies are good with hot coffee or tea, or thick vanilla milkshakes.

16 2-by-2-inch blondies

½ cup plus 2 tablespoons unsifted all-purpose flour
2 tablespoons unsifted cake flour
¼ teaspoon baking powder
¼ teaspoon baking soda
¼ teaspoon salt
½ teaspoon freshly grated nutmeg

7 tablespoons unsalted butter, melted and cooled
⅔ cup light brown sugar
2 tablespoons granulated sugar
1 extra-large egg
1 teaspoon vanilla extract
¾ cup sweetened flaked coconut

Preheat the oven to 325 degrees. Butter and flour an 8-by-8-by-2-inch baking pan.

Thoroughly mix the all-purpose flour, cake flour, baking powder, baking soda, salt and nutmeg in a bowl.

Whisk the butter, brown sugar, granulated sugar, egg and vanilla extract in a bowl. Pour the butter-sugar mixture over the dry ingredients, add the coconut and stir to form a batter.

Pour and scrape the batter into the prepared pan; spread the batter evenly. Bake the blondies for 22 to 25 minutes, or until just set.

Cool the blondies completely in the pan on a rack. Cut into 2-by-2-inch squares. Remove the blondies from the pan using a metal spatula. Store in an airtight tin.

VARIATIONS

For *Coconut Blondies with Chocolate Chips*, toss ½ cup miniature semi-sweet chocolate chips with 1 teaspoon of the flour mixture and add to the batter along with the coconut.

For *Coconut Blondies with Butterscotch Chips*, toss ½ cup butterscotch chips with 1 teaspoon of the flour mixture, and add to the batter along with the coconut.

Chocolate Chip Butterscotch Blondies

These blondies are good to keep on hand in the cookie tin, or to make in large quantities for a charity or school bake sale. Miniature semisweet chocolate chips, or chopped bittersweet candy bars (such as Lindt Excellence or Tobler Tradition) are both fine substitutes for regular chocolate chips.

16 2¼-by-2¼-inch blondies

¾ cup unsifted all-purpose flour
¼ cup unsifted cake flour
¼ teaspoon baking powder
½ teaspoon salt
1 cup semisweet chocolate chips
8 tablespoons (1 stick) unsalted
  butter, melted and cooled

1 cup light brown sugar
¼ cup granulated sugar
1 extra-large egg
2 extra-large egg yolks
2 teaspoons vanilla extract

Preheat the oven to 350 degrees. Butter and flour a 9-by-9-by-2-inch baking pan.

Thoroughly mix the all-purpose flour, cake flour, baking powder and salt in a bowl. Toss the chocolate chips with 2 teaspoons of the flour mixture.

Whisk the butter, light brown sugar, granulated sugar, egg, egg yolks and vanilla extract in a bowl. Pour the butter-sugar mixture over the dry ingredients, add the chocolate chips and stir to form a batter.

Pour and scrape the batter into the prepared pan; spread the batter evenly. Bake the blondies for 25 to 29 minutes, or until just set and pale golden on top.

Cool the blondies completely in the pan on a rack. Cut into 2¼-by-2¼-inch squares. Remove the blondies from the pan using a metal spatula. Store in an airtight tin.

VARIATIONS

For *Chocolate Chip Butterscotch Blondies with Walnuts or Pecans*, add ½ cup chopped nuts to the batter along with the chocolate chips.

For *Chocolate Chip Butterscotch Blondies with Coconut*, add ⅓ cup shredded coconut to the batter along with the chocolate chips.

Peanut Butter "Candy" Blondies

Chopped chocolate-covered peanut butter patties add a sweet topnote to these blondies, which are thicker and richer than the Classic Peanut Butter Blondies on page 66. The baked blondies can be frosted with the dark chocolate icing on page 24, if you wish.

16 2¼-by-2¼-inch blondies

1½ cups unsifted all-purpose flour
1 teaspoon baking powder
¼ teaspoon salt
2 packages (1.8 ounces each) milk
  chocolate peanut butter cups,
  coarsely chopped (see Note)
5 tablespoons unsalted butter,
  melted and cooled

2 tablespoons shortening, melted
  and cooled
½ cup light brown sugar
⅓ cup granulated sugar
½ cup creamy peanut butter
2 extra-large eggs
1 teaspoon vanilla extract
½ cup chopped walnuts

Preheat the oven to 350 degrees. Butter and flour a 9-by-9-by-2-inch baking pan.

Thoroughly mix the all-purpose flour, baking powder and salt. Toss the candy with 1½ teaspoons of the flour mixture.

Beat the butter, shortening, light brown sugar, granulated sugar and peanut butter in the large bowl of an electric mixer on moderate speed for 3 minutes; beat in the eggs, one at a time, blending well after each addition. Blend in the vanilla extract. Add the dry ingredients and stir to form a batter. Stir in the candy and walnuts.

Pour and scrape the batter into the prepared pan; spread the batter evenly. Bake the blondies for 25 minutes, or until just set.

Cool the blondies completely in the pan on a rack. Cut into 2¼-by-2¼-inch squares. Remove the blondies from the pan using a metal spatula. Store in an airtight tin.

NOTE: 2 bars (1.7 ounces each) chocolate-covered peanut and toasted coconut candy, chopped, can be substituted for the peanut butter patties.

Cashew and Peanut Butter Blondies

The small amount of oatmeal added to the batter gives this blondie an earthy, substantial texture. These blondies are very good served with warm-from-the-oven baked apples.

16 2¼-by-2¼-inch blondies

¾ cup unsifted all-purpose flour
¼ cup unsifted cake flour
¼ teaspoon baking soda
¼ teaspoon salt
6 tablespoons unsalted butter,
    softened at room temperature
½ cup creamy peanut butter
¾ cup light brown sugar

½ cup granulated sugar
1 extra-large egg
2 extra-large egg yolks
1½ teaspoons vanilla extract
⅓ cup "quick-cooking" (not
    instant) oatmeal
¾ cup chopped cashews

Preheat the oven to 350 degrees. Butter and flour a 9-by-9-by-2-inch baking pan.

Thoroughly mix the all-purpose flour, cake flour, baking soda and salt.

Beat the butter, peanut butter, brown sugar and granulated sugar in the large bowl of an electric mixer on moderate speed for 3 minutes. Beat in the eggs, egg yolks and vanilla extract. Stir in the dry ingredients, oatmeal and cashews.

Pour and scrape the batter into the prepared pan; spread the batter evenly. Bake the blondies for 25 minutes, or until just set.

Cool the blondies completely in the pan on a rack. Cut into 2¼-by-2¼-inch squares. Remove the blondies from the pan using a metal spatula. Store in an airtight tin.

Date and Walnut Blondies

A plate of Date and Walnut Blondies is a satisfying autumn treat, teamed with hot tea, apple cider or mulled wine.

16 2¼-by-2¼-inch blondies

1 cup unsifted all-purpose flour
¼ cup unsifted cake flour
½ teaspoon baking soda
½ teaspoon baking powder
¼ teaspoon salt
½ teaspoon freshly grated nutmeg
¼ teaspoon ground cinnamon
6 tablespoons unsalted butter, melted and cooled

3 tablespoons shortening, melted and cooled
1 cup light brown sugar
¼ cup superfine sugar
1 extra-large egg
1½ teaspoons vanilla extract
1 cup chopped walnuts
⅔ cup chopped pitted dates

Preheat the oven to 350 degrees. Lightly butter and flour a 9-by-9-by-2-inch baking pan.

Thoroughly mix the all-purpose flour, cake flour, baking soda, baking powder, salt, nutmeg and cinnamon in a bowl.

Whisk the butter, shortening, brown sugar, superfine sugar, egg and vanilla extract in a bowl. Pour the butter-sugar mixture over the dry ingredients, add the walnuts and dates, and stir to form a batter. The batter will be fairly stiff.

Pour and scrape the batter into the prepared pan; spread the batter evenly. Bake the blondies for 30 to 33 minutes, or until just set.

Cool the blondies completely in the pan on a rack. Cut into 2¼-by-¼-inch squares. Remove the blondies from the pan using a metal spatula. Store in an airtight tin.

Granola Blondies

These blondies are endowed with a handful of granola, flaked coconut, chopped walnuts, sunflower seeds and raisins. Stirring in ½ cup butterscotch morsels would make them sweeter and richer.

16 2-by-2-inch blondies

⅔ cup unsifted all-purpose flour
¼ teaspoon baking powder
¼ teaspoon salt
1½ teaspoons ground cinnamon
½ teaspoon freshly grated nutmeg
Pinch ground allspice
¼ cup chopped walnuts
¼ cup dark raisins
2 tablespoons roasted sunflower seeds
8 tablespoons (1 stick) unsalted butter, melted and cooled

1 tablespoon shortening, melted and cooled
⅔ cup light brown sugar
3 tablespoons granulated sugar
1 extra-large egg
1 teaspoon vanilla extract
¼ teaspoon almond extract
1 cup granola
¼ cup sweetened flaked coconut

Preheat the oven to 350 degrees. Lightly butter and flour an 8-by-8-by-2-inch baking pan.

Thoroughly mix the all-purpose flour, baking powder, salt, cinnamon, nutmeg and allspice in a bowl. Toss the walnuts, raisins and sunflower seeds with 1 tablespoon of the flour mixture.

Whisk the butter, shortening, brown sugar, granulated sugar, egg, vanilla extract and almond extract in a bowl. Pour the butter-sugar mixture over the dry ingredients, add the granola, coconut, walnuts, raisins and sunflower seeds, and stir to form a batter.

Pour and scrape the batter into the prepared pan; spread the batter evenly. Bake the blondies in the preheated oven for 25 minutes, or until just set.

Cool the blondies completely in the pan on a rack. Cut into 2-by-2-inch squares. Remove the blondies from the pan with a metal spatula. Store in an airtight tin.

Currant, Oatmeal and Pecan Blondies

These blondies remind me of lush oatmeal cookies, for they are plain, soft and slightly chewy. Serve the blondies with a fruit salad, or on their own with coffee, tea or apple cider.

16 2¼-by-2¼-inch blondies

1 cup unsifted all-purpose flour
½ cup unsifted cake flour
1 teaspoon baking powder
¼ teaspoon salt
1 teaspoon ground cinnamon
½ teaspoon freshly grated nutmeg
½ cup moist dried currants
8 tablespoons (1 stick) unsalted
    butter, melted and cooled

1 cup light brown sugar
¼ cup granulated sugar
2 extra-large eggs
1½ teaspoons vanilla extract
½ cup "quick-cooking" (not
    instant) oatmeal
½ cup sweetened flaked coconut
½ cup chopped pecans

Preheat the oven to 350 degrees. Butter and flour a 9-by-9-by-2-inch baking pan.

Thoroughly mix the all-purpose flour, cake flour, baking powder, salt, cinnamon and nutmeg in a bowl. Toss the currants with 1 teaspoon of the flour mixture.

Whisk the butter, brown sugar, granulated sugar, eggs and vanilla extract in a bowl. Pour the butter-sugar mixture over the dry ingredients, add the oatmeal, coconut, pecans and currants, and stir to form a batter.

Scrape the batter into the prepared pan; spread the batter evenly. Bake the blondies for 25 minutes, or until just set.

Cool the blondies completely in the pan on a rack. Cut into 2¼-by-2¼-inch squares. Remove the blondies from the pan using a metal spatula. Store in an airtight tin.

VARIATION

For *Raisin, Oatmeal and Pecan Blondies*, substitute dark or golden raisins for the currants.

Toffee Blondies

These blondies are filled with chopped toffee candy and semisweet chocolate morsels, and topped with chopped almonds. Rich and chewy, they are an ideal companion to coffee, tea or hot chocolate.

30 1¾-by 2¼-inch blondies

1⅔ cups unsifted all-purpose flour
⅓ cup unsifted cake flour
1¾ teaspoons baking powder
½ teaspoon salt
¼ cup semisweet chocolate chips
14 tablespoons (1 stick plus
    6 tablespoons) unsalted butter,
    melted and cooled
1 cup light brown sugar

1 cup granulated sugar
2 extra-large eggs
2 extra-large egg yolks
2 teaspoons vanilla extract
6 bars (1.4 ounces each)
    chocolate-covered toffee candy,
    chopped
½ cup chopped almonds

Preheat the oven to 350 degrees. Butter and flour a 13-by-9-by-2-inch baking pan.

Thoroughly mix the all-purpose flour, cake flour, baking powder and salt in a bowl. Toss the chocolate chips with 2 teaspoons of this mixture.

Whisk the butter, brown sugar, granulated sugar, eggs, egg yolks and vanilla extract. Pour the butter-sugar mixture over the dry ingredients and stir to form a batter. Stir in the toffee and chocolate chips.

Pour and scrape the batter into the prepared pan; spread the batter evenly. Sprinkle the almonds on top.

Bake the blondies for 30 minutes. Cool the blondies completely in the pan on a rack. Cut into 1¾-by-2¼-inch rectangles. Remove the blondies from the pan using a metal spatula. Store in an airtight tin.

Spiced Oatmeal and Coconut Blondies

The oatmeal batter serves as a soft and chewy cushion for strands of coconut and plump raisins; these blondies are good to have on hand for tucking into the lunch box.

16 2-by-2-inch blondies

1 cup unsifted all-purpose flour
½ teaspoon baking soda
¼ teaspoon salt
¾ teaspoon ground cinnamon
½ teaspoon freshly grated nutmeg
¼ teaspoon ground ginger
½ cup dark raisins
8 tablespoons (1 stick) unsalted
    butter, softened

½ cup light brown sugar
½ cup granulated sugar
1 extra-large egg
1 teaspoon vanilla extract
¾ cup "quick-cooking" (not
    instant) oatmeal
½ cup sweetened flaked coconut

Preheat the oven to 350 degrees. Butter and flour an 8-by-8-by-2-inch baking pan.

Thoroughly mix the all-purpose flour, baking soda, salt, cinnamon, nutmeg and ginger. Toss the raisins with 1 teaspoon of the flour mixture.

Beat the butter, brown sugar and granulated sugar in the large bowl of an electric mixer on moderate speed for 3 minutes; beat in the egg and vanilla extract. Stir in the dry ingredients, oatmeal, coconut and raisins.

Pour and scrape the batter into the prepared pan; spread the batter evenly. Bake the blondies for 30 minutes, or until just set.

Cool the blondies completely in the pan on a rack. Cut into 2-by-2-inch squares. Remove the blondies from the pan using a metal spatula. Store in an airtight tin.

Sour Cream and Almond Blondies

The sour cream in the batter creates a very moist, slightly dense blondie. If you wish, a half cup of butterscotch or miniature semisweet chocolate morsels, or one 3-ounce bar of bittersweet chocolate, chopped, can be stirred into the batter at the last moment, along with the almonds.

16 2¼-by-2¼-inch blondies

1 cup unsifted all-purpose flour	6 tablespoons unsalted butter,
¼ cup unsifted cake flour	melted and cooled
¼ teaspoon baking soda	1 cup light brown sugar
¼ teaspoon salt	⅓ cup sour cream
¼ teaspoon ground cinnamon	1 teaspoon vanilla extract
¼ teaspoon freshly grated nutmeg	¼ teaspoon almond extract
1 extra-large egg	1 cup chopped almonds

Preheat the oven to 350 degrees. Butter and flour a 9-by-9-by-2-inch baking pan.

Thoroughly mix the all-purpose flour, cake flour, baking soda, salt, cinnamon and nutmeg in a bowl.

Whisk the egg and butter in a bowl; beat in the sugar, sour cream, and vanilla and almond extracts. Pour the butter-sugar mixture over the dry ingredients, add the almonds and stir to form a batter.

Pour and scrape the batter into the prepared pan; spread the batter evenly. Bake the blondies for 27 minutes, or until just set.

Cool the blondies completely in the pan on a rack. Cut into 2¼-by-2¼-inch squares. Remove the blondies from the pan using a metal spatula. Store in an airtight tin, separating the layers with sheets of wax paper.

Golden Pecan Blondies

The brown sugar adds a rounded caramel flavor to these nutty squares. As satisfying as they are rich, the blondies are good with hot lemon tea, cold glasses of lemonade, limeade or small cups of espresso.

30 1¾-by-2¼-inch blondies

1½ cups unsifted all-purpose flour
½ cup unsifted cake flour
½ teaspoon baking powder
½ teaspoon salt
14 tablespoons (1 stick plus
    6 tablespoons) unsalted butter,
    melted and cooled
3 tablespoons shortening, melted
    and cooled

1 cup light brown sugar
½ cup granulated sugar
2 extra-large eggs
2 extra-large egg yolks
1½ teaspoons vanilla extract
1½ cups chopped pecans
⅔ cup sweetened flaked coconut

Preheat the oven to 350 degrees. Butter and flour a 13-by-9-by-2-inch baking pan.

Thoroughly mix the all-purpose flour, cake flour, baking powder and salt in a bowl.

Whisk the butter, shortening, brown sugar and granulated sugar in a bowl; beat in the eggs, egg yolks and vanilla extract. Pour the butter-sugar mixture over the dry ingredients, add the pecans and coconut and stir.

Pour and scrape the batter into the prepared pan; spread the batter evenly. Bake the blondies for 28 to 30 minutes, or until just set.

Cool the blondies completely in the pan on a rack. Cut into 1¾-by-2¼-inch rectangles. Remove the blondies from the pan using a metal spatula. Store in an airtight tin.

Oatmeal and Peanut Butter Blondies

Think of this recipe as a basic design for a chewy, butterscotch- and peanut butter-flavored blondie: raisins or currants, chopped peanuts or whole chocolate-covered peanuts, or butterscotch chips are all possible additions.

16 2¼-by-2¼-inch blondies

1¼ cups unsifted all-purpose flour
¾ teaspoon baking soda
¼ teaspoon salt
½ teaspoon freshly grated nutmeg
8 tablespoons (1 stick) unsalted butter, melted and cooled
1 tablespoon shortening, melted and cooled
¾ cup light brown sugar

½ cup granulated sugar
¾ cup creamy peanut butter
3 tablespoons milk
2 extra-large eggs
1 teaspoon vanilla extract
1 cup "quick-cooking" (not instant) oatmeal
½ cup sweetened flaked coconut

Preheat the oven to 350 degrees. Butter and flour a 9-by-9-by-2-inch baking pan.

Thoroughly mix the all-purpose flour, baking soda, salt and nutmeg.

Whisk the butter, shortening, brown sugar and granulated sugar in a bowl; add the peanut butter and beat for 2 minutes. Blend in the milk. Beat in the eggs, one at a time, beating well after each addition; blend in the vanilla extract. Add the dry ingredients, oatmeal and coconut, and stir.

Pour and scrape the batter into the prepared pan; spread the batter evenly. Bake the blondies for 30 minutes, or until just set.

Cool the blondies completely in the pan on a rack. Cut into 2¼-by-2¼-inch squares. Remove the blondies from the pan using a metal spatula. Store in an airtight tin.

Bittersweet Chocolate and Coconut Blondies

These chewy blondies are thickset with bits of chocolate and walnuts. Miniature semisweet chocolate chips, tossed in a few teaspoons of the flour mixture, can be substituted for the chopped bittersweet bar.

16 2¼-by-2¼-inch blondies

¾ cup unsifted all-purpose flour
¼ cup unsifted cake flour
½ teaspoon baking powder
¼ teaspoon salt
2 bars (3 ounces each) bittersweet
   chocolate, chopped
8 tablespoons (1 stick) unsalted
   butter, melted and cooled

½ cup light brown sugar
½ cup granulated sugar
2 extra-large eggs
1 teaspoon vanilla extract
¾ cup chopped walnuts

Preheat the oven to 350 degrees. Butter and flour a 9-by-9-by-2-inch baking pan.

Thoroughly mix the all-purpose flour, cake flour, baking powder and salt. Toss the chocolate with 2 teaspoons of the flour mixture.

Whisk the butter, brown sugar and granulated sugar in a mixing bowl; beat in the eggs and vanilla extract. Add the dry ingredients and stir to form a batter. Stir in the chocolate and ½ cup walnuts.

Pour and scrape the batter into the prepared pan. Sprinkle the remaining walnuts on top. Bake the blondies for 28 minutes, or until just set.

Cool the blondies completely in the pan on a rack. Cut into 2¼-by-2¼-inch squares. Remove the blondies from the pan using a metal spatula. Store in an airtight tin.

Banana Blondies

Nibble on these soft, fine-textured blondies at teatime, or serve them for dessert with a fresh or stewed fruit compote.

16 2-by-2-inch blondies

1 large ripe banana
¾ cup unsifted all-purpose flour
½ teaspoon baking powder
¼ teaspoon salt
½ teaspoon ground cinnamon
¼ teaspoon freshly grated nutmeg

5 tablespoons unsalted butter,
  melted and cooled
⅔ cup light brown sugar
1 extra-large egg
½ teaspoon vanilla extract
½ cup chopped walnuts

Preheat the oven to 350 degrees. Butter and flour an 8-by-8-by-2-inch baking pan.

Mash the banana with a fork; there should be a scant ¾ cup.

Thoroughly mix the all-purpose flour, baking powder, salt, cinnamon and nutmeg in a bowl.

Whisk the butter, sugar, egg and vanilla extract in a bowl; stir in the banana. Pour the butter-sugar-banana mixture over the dry ingredients, and stir to form a batter. Stir in the walnuts.

Pour and scrape the batter into the prepared pan; spread the batter evenly. Bake the blondies for 30 minutes, or until just set.

Cool the blondies completely in the pan on a rack. Cut into 2-by-2-inch squares. Remove the blondies from the pan using a metal spatula. Store in an airtight tin.

VARIATIONS

For *Banana Blondies with Dates*, add ½ cup chopped, pitted dates to the batter along with the walnuts.

For *Banana Blondies with Raisins*, add ½ cup dark raisins to the batter along with the walnuts.

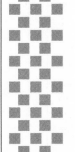

Spiced Applesauce Blondies

The applesauce and shredded apple in this batter keeps these homestyle blondies moist. Plain, cakelike and gently flavored with spices, the squares are ideal to serve with hot cider, mulled wine or coffee.

16 2¼-by-2¼-inch blondies

¾ cup unsifted all-purpose flour
½ cup unsifted cake flour
½ teaspoon baking powder
¼ teaspoon baking soda
¼ teaspoon salt
½ teaspoon ground cinnamon
¼ teaspoon freshly grated nutmeg
¼ teaspoon ground allspice
8 tablespoons (1 stick) unsalted
   butter, melted and cooled

½ cup light brown sugar
⅓ cup granulated sugar
2 extra-large eggs
¾ teaspoon vanilla extract
¼ cup unsweetened applesauce
1 tart cooking apple, peeled, cored
   and shredded (use the large
   holes of a hand grater)
⅔ cup chopped walnuts

Preheat the oven to 350 degrees. Butter and flour a 9-by-9-by-2-inch baking pan.

Thoroughly mix the all-purpose flour, cake flour, baking powder, baking soda, salt, cinnamon, nutmeg and allspice in a bowl.

Whisk the butter, brown sugar, granulated sugar, eggs and vanilla extract in a bowl; blend in the applesauce and shredded apple. Pour the butter–sugar–apple mixture over the dry ingredients, and stir to form a batter. Stir in the walnuts.

Pour and scrape the batter into the prepared pan; spread the batter evenly. Bake the blondies for 30 minutes, or until just set.

Cool the blondies completely in the pan on a rack. Cut into 2¼-by-2¼-inch squares. Remove the blondies from the pan using a metal spatula. Store in an airtight tin.

VARIATIONS

For *Applesauce Blondies with Raisins*, toss ¾ cup golden or dark raisins with 2 teaspoons of the flour mixture. Add the raisins to the batter along with the walnuts.

For *Applesauce Blondies with Pecans*, substitute pecans for the walnuts.

Maple Blondies with Golden Raisins and Pecans

These blondies are good on their own, or served with plain fruit desserts, such as warm baked apples, applesauce, poached pears, or stewed dried fruit.

30 1¾-by-2¼-inch blondies

2 cups unsifted all-purpose flour
¾ teaspoon baking powder
¼ teaspoon baking soda
¾ teaspoon salt
¾ teaspoon ground cinnamon
½ teaspoon freshly grated nutmeg
½ teaspoon ground allspice
½ cup golden raisins
12 tablespoons (1 stick plus
   4 tablespoons) unsalted butter,
   melted and cooled

4 tablespoons shortening, melted
   and cooled
1 cup light brown sugar
¼ cup granulated sugar
3 extra-large eggs
¼ cup pure maple syrup
1 teaspoon vanilla extract
1¼ cups chopped pecans

Preheat the oven to 350 degrees. Butter and flour a 13-by-9-by-2-inch baking pan.

Thoroughly mix the all-purpose flour, baking powder, baking soda, salt, cinnamon, nutmeg and allspice in a bowl. Toss the raisins with 2 teaspoons of the flour mixture.

Whisk the butter, shortening, brown sugar, granulated sugar and eggs in a bowl; beat in the maple syrup and vanilla extract. Pour the butter–

sugar–maple syrup mixture over the dry ingredients, and stir to form a batter. Stir in the pecans and raisins.

Pour and scrape the batter into the prepared pan; spread the batter evenly. Bake the blondies for 27 to 30 minutes, or until just set and golden on top.

Cool the blondies completely in the pan on a rack. Cut into 1¾-by-2¼-inch rectangles. Remove the blondies from the pan using a metal spatula. Store in an airtight tin.

Apricot Blondies

The combination of dried apricots and apricot preserves gives this blondie batter a sweet-tart tang.

30 1¾-by-2¼-inch blondies

¾ cup dried apricots
1½ cups unsifted all-purpose flour
½ cup unsifted cake flour
½ teaspoon baking soda
½ teaspoon salt
1 teaspoon freshly grated nutmeg
1 cup light brown sugar

2 tablespoons granulated sugar
½ pound (2 sticks) unsalted
   butter, melted and cooled
2 tablespoons apricot preserves
2 extra-large eggs
1 extra-large egg yolk
1 cup chopped walnuts

Preheat the oven to 350 degrees. Butter and flour a 13-by-9-by-2-inch baking pan.

Place the apricots in a bowl, pour over enough hot water to cover, and let the fruit soften in the water for 10 minutes; drain the apricots well, pat dry on paper towels and chop coarsely.

Thoroughly mix the all-purpose flour, cake flour, baking soda, salt and nutmeg in a bowl.

Whisk the brown sugar, granulated sugar, butter, apricot preserves, eggs and egg yolk in a bowl. Pour the butter-sugar mixture over the dry ingredients and stir to form a batter. Stir in the apricots and walnuts.

Pour and scrape the batter into the prepared pan; spread the batter evenly. Bake the blondies for 30 minutes, or until just set.

Cool the blondies completely in the pan on a rack. Cut into 1¾-by-2¼-inch rectangles. Remove the blondies from the pan using a metal spatula. Store in an airtight tin.

Rum Raisin Blondies

Rum-soaked raisins add a mellow richness to a panful of blondies. Offer the blondies at teatime, or serve them for dessert topped with scoops of vanilla ice cream.

16 2¼-by-2¼-inch blondies

¾ cup dark raisins
2 tablespoons dark rum
1 cup unsifted all-purpose flour
¼ teaspoon baking powder
¼ teaspoon salt
¼ teaspoon ground cinnamon
¼ teaspoon freshly grated nutmeg

¼ teaspoon ground ginger
8 tablespoons (1 stick) unsalted
   butter, melted and cooled
½ cup light brown sugar
¼ cup granulated sugar
2 extra-large eggs
½ teaspoon vanilla extract

Preheat the oven to 350 degrees. Butter and flour a 9-by-9-by-2-inch baking pan.

Place the raisins in a bowl, add the rum, stir and let stand for a few minutes.

Thoroughly mix the all-purpose flour, baking powder, salt, cinnamon, nutmeg and ginger in a bowl.

Whisk the butter, light brown sugar, granulated sugar, eggs and vanilla extract in a bowl. Blend in the rum-soaked raisins. Pour the butter–sugar–raisin mixture over the dry ingredients, and stir to form a batter.

Pour and scrape the batter into the prepared pan; spread the batter evenly. Bake the blondies for 25 minutes, or until just set.

Cool the blondies completely in the pan on a rack. Cut into 2¼-by-2¼-inch squares. Remove the blondies from the pan using a metal spatula. Store in an airtight tin.

Gingered Walnut Blondies

Bake these blondies in the autumn, when fresh, crisp walnuts appear at the market in time for holiday baking. Full-flavored and nutty, the squares are superb served with caramel ice cream, a prune or apricot compote, or cinnamon-poached apples.

16 2-by-2-inch blondies

1 cup unsifted all-purpose flour
¼ teaspoon baking powder
¼ teaspoon salt
¾ teaspoon ground ginger
6 tablespoons unsalted butter, melted and cooled
½ cup light brown sugar

¼ cup granulated sugar
1 extra-large egg
1 teaspoon vanilla extract
2 tablespoons chopped crystallized ginger
¾ cup chopped walnuts

Preheat the oven to 350 degrees. Butter and flour an 8-by-8-by-2-inch baking pan.

Thoroughly mix the all-purpose flour, baking powder, salt and ground ginger in a bowl.

Whisk the butter, brown sugar, granulated sugar, egg and vanilla extract in a bowl. Pour the butter–sugar mixture over the dry ingredients, and stir to form a batter. Stir in the crystallized ginger and walnuts.

Pour and scrape the batter into the prepared pan; spread the batter evenly. Bake the blondies for 25 minutes, or until just set.

Cool the blondies completely in the pan on a rack. Cut into 2-by-2-inch squares. Remove the blondies from the pan using a metal spatula. Store in an airtight tin.

· 4 ·

Brownies and Blondies for Gift-Giving

PACKAGING THE HANDMADE SWEETS

Brownies and blondies are ideal confections to package for gift-giving, for they can be wrapped individually and nestled in a variety of containers.

Wrap each brownie or blondie in a square of clear cellophane or heavy plastic wrap and seal, making sure that the seams and end flaps are concealed on the underside. The wrapped sweets are ready to layer in cookie tins, baskets or colorful bags.

For a festive look, line the inside of a basket or tin with fresh galax leaves, a length of fabric, fluffs of tulle, several doilies or a downy nest of curly Spanish moss before you layer in the brownies. Bright, pliant strands of ivy or eucalyptus can be used to decorate the outside of a basket; wind the greenery around the basket and secure in spots with thin, flexible florist's wire.

A "brownie basket," filled with a stack of brownies or blondies, makes a fine hostess gift or an attractive addition to the holiday dessert table.

Index